Hello, I am Queen Elizabeth of England. The year is 1577.

My father was King Henry VIII, my mother was Anne Boleyn. My parents' relationship was not good and my father had my mother beheaded when I was three. When my father died, my half brother Edward became king. He was always sickly and died at 16. Then my half-sister, Mary Tudor, became Queen. Mary married the Spanish Prince Philip who would eventually become King Philip II of Spain. For a time Philip lived in England but as Mary did not have children, he left. Mary is remembered in history as "Bloody Mary" for her persecution of Protestants. Between 1555 and 1558, she ordered about 300 Protestants to be burned at the stake. On Mary's death, I became the Queen in 1558.

I have worked hard to be a popular Queen. Under my rule England is enjoying a golden age of exploration, art, music, and literature. It is 85 years since Christopher Columbus sailed to the New World and discovered the West Indian (Caribbean) islands. Between 1492 and 1504 Spain conquered the Aztec Empire, then moved south to conquer Peru and the west coast of Chile. Spain has grown rich from gold and silver mines in the New World and her treasure ships carry vast wealth home to Spain. If I can disrupt Spain's power here, I can take some of this wealth for England!

Spices worth more than their weight in gold come from the East by a long overland journey. For years there has been talk of a shorter sea route, the so called North West Passage to the Spice Islands. The country that finds this route, (if it exists), will be very powerful indeed. Francis Drake is the right commander for this expedition! His reputation as a pirate is the perfect cover for the voyage. If anything goes wrong I will deny everything to avoid a war with Spain.

Author:
David Stewart has written many non-fiction books for children on historical topics, including *You Wouldn't Want to Be an Egyptian Mummy* and *You Wouldn't Want to Sail on the Titanic*. He lives in Brighton with his wife and son.

Artist:
David Antram was born in Brighton, England, in 1958. He studied at Eastbourne College of Art and then worked in advertising for fifteen years before becoming a full-time artist. He has illustrated many children's non-fiction books.

Series Creator:
David Salariya was born in Dundee, Scotland. He has illustrated a wide range of books and has created and designed many new series for publishers both in the UK and overseas. In 1989, he established The Salariya Book Company. He lives in Brighton with his wife, illustrator Shirley Willis, and their son Jonathan.

Consultant:
Stuart Slade read film and literature at Warwick University and gained a postgraduate diploma in Museum Studies at the University of Leicester in 1991. He has worked as Education Officer at the National Maritime Museum since 1998, developing a range of programmes and resources for primary, secondary and college groups, including many on Tudor exploration.

Editor: **Karen Smith**

© The Salariya Book Company Ltd MMV

Published in Great Britain in 2005 by
Book House, an imprint of
The Salariya Book Company Ltd
25 Marlborough Place, Brighton BN1 1UB

Please visit the Salariya Book Company at:
www.salariya.com

ISBN 0-531-12413-4 (Lib. Bdg.)
ISBN 0-531-12393-6 (Pbk.)

Published in 2005 in the United States
by Franklin Watts
An imprint of Scholastic Library Publishing
90 Sherman Turnpike, Danbury, CT 06816

A CIP catalog record for this title is available from the Library of Congress.

Printed and bound in China.
Manufactured by Leo Paper Products Ltd.
Printed on paper from sustainable forests.

You Wouldn't Want to Explore With Sir Francis Drake!

Be warned: if anyone hits a shipmate, they will lose their head!

A Pirate You'd Rather Not Know

Written by
David Stewart

Illustrated by
David Antram

Created and designed by
David Salariya

Franklin Watts®
A Division of Scholastic Inc.
NEW YORK • TORONTO • LONDON • AUCKLAND • SYDNEY
MEXICO CITY • NEW DELHI • HONG KONG
DANBURY, CONNECTICUT

Contents

Introduction

t is 1577 and Francis Drake, the Queen of England's favorite adventurer, has been ordered to command a new expedition leaving from Plymouth. You are Francis Fletcher, a young preacher. You have heard stories about Drake's raids on ships along the coast of South America. Drake is a deeply religious man and you have the good luck to be appointed as Chaplain to the expedition. You believe you are off on a trading trip to Alexandria in Egypt, but Drake's expedition has another purpose. Where will this voyage take you? You will return from your journey nearly three years later a well-traveled and wiser man. But you certainly wouldn't want to explore with Francis Drake again!

I am Francis Drake. Some say I am a pirate!

Pirate or Privateer?

Francis Fletcher

YOU ARE A GRADUATE of Cambridge University and an experienced traveler. You've already visited Russia, Spain and the Mediterranean.

I am Francis Fletcher. I plan to make notes in my journal of the voyage.

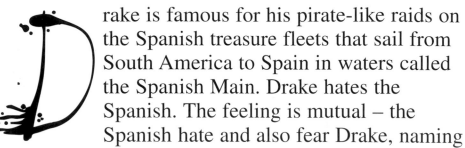

Drake is famous for his pirate-like raids on the Spanish treasure fleets that sail from South America to Spain in waters called the Spanish Main. Drake hates the Spanish. The feeling is mutual – the Spanish hate and also fear Drake, naming him *El Draque* (the dragon). Philip II, the King of Spain, suspects that Drake is a privateer. This would mean that Drake's raids are approved by the Queen and that the Queen profits from them. Little do you know that the huge cost of this new expedition may well be covered by such acts of piracy.

The Spanish Treasure Fleets

THE TREASURE FLEETS sail twice a year from Spain, carrying provisions, food, clothing, wine, oil, and tools to South America. On the return journey the ships are loaded with silver and gold.

Handy Hint

Sail with an experienced captain. Drake has made many voyages.

MEXICO

Caribbean Sea

SOUTH AMERICA

The Spanish Main

THE SPANISH TREASURE FLEET must sail through the Spanish Main on their voyages between the New World and Spain. Pirates are attracted to this region by these rich ships and the numerous islands and bays in which to hide.

DRAKE comes from a family of seafarers. Long ago, William Hawkins, Drake's uncle, showed King Henry VIII exotic fruit he had brought back from his travels.

So, these coconuts, bananas and oranges — what do you do with them?

The Queen's Secret Plans

Y ou think you're on an expedition in search of the Northwest Passage, a possible sea route between the Atlantic and Pacific Oceans. Drake has chosen the *Pelican* as his flagship, a 120-ton, 18-gun ship with a double hull, built with Drake's own money. One hundred sixty four men and boys make up the crew, some of whom invested money in the expedition. Thomas Doughty is one of them.

On November 15, 1577, the *Pelican* sails from Plymouth with four other ships: the *Elizabeth*, the *Marigold*, the *Swan,* and the *Benedict*. However, wild storms soon force the ships back to Plymouth and some are badly damaged. On December 13 the expedition sets sail once more for the Moroccan island of Mogador.

The Real Purpose of the Expedition Is Revealed!

LIKE MOST OF THE CREW you think you are on a trading mission to the Nile in Alexandria. On reaching the coast of Africa, your destination changes.

YOUR REAL DESTINATION is the Pacific Ocean via the Strait of Magellan to find the Northwest Passage – the route to the Far East and the fabled Spice Islands.

SOME OF THE CREW are not happy about the change of plan. Of course, if you can raid the Spanish treasure fleet and take some of Spain's treasure, that would be nice.

YOUR SMALL FLEET CAPTURES a Portuguese ship near São Tiago in the Cape Verde Islands. One of the prisoners, Nuño De Silva, is an experienced navigator. When he hears where you are going he chooses to come with you. He has useful maps and charts which are more valuable than gold to Drake.

Handy Hint

Aching and swollen joints? Bad breath? Bleeding gums? Teeth falling out? You have scurvy! Eat plenty of fresh fruit.

It's the charts that are important...

Island of Blood

When the ships anchor at Port St. Julian, the crew are uneasy. Thomas Doughty is accused of plotting against Drake and is brought to trial. At his trial, 40 men on the jury find Thomas Doughty guilty and he is sentenced to death for mutiny. Doughty chooses to die under the axe. Drake decides that only three vessels will now sail on from Port St. Julian: the *Pelican* (now re-named the *Golden Hinde*) the *Marigold* and the *Elizabeth*. On August 17, 1578, the ships set sail for the Strait of Magellan.

TALES OF MAGELLAN'S CRUELTY to the native people 58 years earlier have not been forgotten. The native people are not friendly (left). Your gunner and the surgeon are killed in a fight.

CAPTURED during another raid, the *Mary* is too rotten to use any more. The ship is broken up and used as firewood (right).

THE CREW SPEND THEIR TIME "CAREENING" — scraping barnacles and seaweed off the hull to prevent them from slowing the ship down (left). Drake is very careful about the maintenance of his ships.

THE COOPER (barrel-maker) from the *Pelican* makes tankards (right) from the gibbet (wooden frame) used by explorer Magellan to hang his mutinous crew member.

Lo! This is the end of traitors!

Handy Hint

Sea lion oil is good for curing pimples. Eat mussels and seaweed stew to give you strength!

Re-naming the Flagship

The *Pelican* is re-named the *Golden Hinde* on August 21, 1578, in honor of Sir Christopher Hatton, whose crest featured a 'hinde', a female deer. Thomas Doughty was Hatton's private secretary. Drake is hoping to be in Hatton's good graces when he has to explain Doughty's execution.

Storms Hit the Fleet

Golden Hinde's route

NORTH AMERICA

AFRICA

Atlantic Ocean

Peru

SOUTH AMERICA

Precise route unknown!

After sailing through the Strait of Magellan safely, fierce storms rage in the Pacific for two months. The fleet hugs the coast of South America, Drake tries to keep the ships together but the ships become separated. The *Golden Hinde* is blown far to the south. The *Marigold* sinks in the storm with all on board. Drake thinks the *Elizabeth* is lost too. Fifty-two days after the ships have passed through the Strait of Magellan a course is set to sail to Peru.

ENGLISH, FRENCH, Scots, Welsh and other nationalities make up the company of about 88 men and boys on board the *Golden Hinde*.

THE *ELIZABETH* is blown back to the Strait of Magellan and sails for England where she arrives safely.

THE CREW KILLS about 3,000 penguins which gives them enough meat for 40 days. The Welsh men name the flightless birds "pen gwyns" which is Welsh for "white-heads."

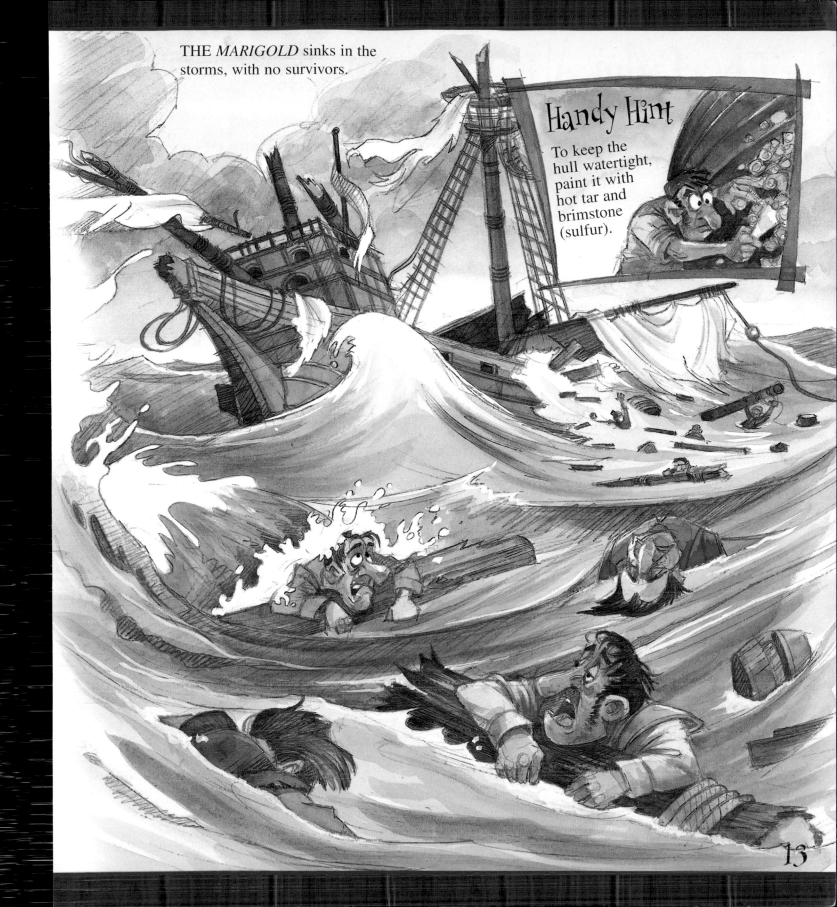

THE *MARIGOLD* sinks in the storms, with no survivors.

Handy Hint

To keep the hull watertight, paint it with hot tar and brimstone (sulfur).

Plundering Treasure Ships

The *Cacafuego* and her crew are set free and the *Golden Hinde* sails 597 miles (960 km) in nine days along the west coast of New Spain (now Central America). Anchored near the island of Caño, the crew enjoys fresh meat for the first time in a month, including monkey and alligator! With treasure piling up in the hold, Drake is on the look-out for another ship to share the load. The *Capitiana* is captured along with its useful navigation charts for a route to Manila in the Philippines. Barnacles are building up on the *Golden Hinde*'s hull which slow her down. She needs to be careened but a partial clean-up has to do. A few weeks later Spanish nobleman Don Francisco de Zárate's ship is sighted.

Please don't take my clothes, they are very expensive.

AT DUSK on April 3 Zárate's ship is sighted on the horizon. The crew board her at dawn and find her full of riches.

THE SHIP IS LADEN with linen, chests full of fine china dishes and oriental silks.

ZÁRATE is finely dressed and pleads with Drake not to take his expensive clothes. Drake takes nearly everything else, including the passengers' trunks!

ZÁRATE IS INVITED TO DINE with Drake on the *Golden Hinde* and later reports that the food was served on "silver dishes given to Drake by the Queen". He also reports that Drake is "about 35 years of age...with a fair beard, and is one of the greatest mariners that sails the seas". When Drake escorts Zárate back to his ship, he leaves the Portuguese pilot behind, too.

Handy Hint

To persuade a captured pilot to steer your ship through unknown waters threaten to hang him.

Here's to the Queen of England, God bless her.

17

Making Repairs

rake's small fleet sails west and then north. By mid-July the ships are in need of repair so a safe harbor must be found. They anchor in a bay which Drake names 'Nova Albion', Latin meaning 'New England'. Today that would be somewhere on the Californian coast. The native people seem peaceful. Some of the crew go hunting with the native people and discover they are very skillful with bows and arrows.

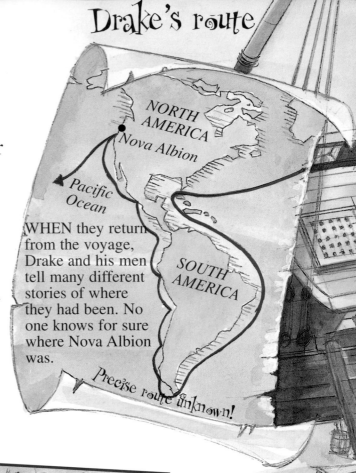

Drake's route

NORTH AMERICA

Nova Albion

Pacific Ocean

SOUTH AMERICA

WHEN they return from the voyage, Drake and his men tell many different stories of where they had been. No one knows for sure where Nova Albion was.

Precise route unknown!

Nova Albion

THE *GOLDEN HINDE* is leaking. It is too bitterly cold and stormy to go further north in search of the fabled Northwest Passage.

IN THE SHALLOW BAY they named Nova Albion careening and vital repairs are done to the ship.

FIVE WEEKS PASS in this safe harbor. Drake leaves an engraved brass plate nailed to a post, claiming the land for Queen Elizabeth.

Handy Hint

You may not like it but take all the advice you can from the locals. They know this place best.

I claim this land for Queen Elizabeth, the Queen of England.

The Island of Thieves

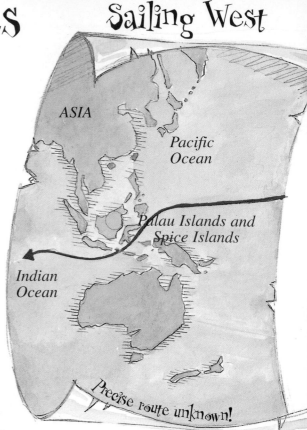

ASIA

Pacific
Ocean

Palau Islands and
Spice Islands

Indian
Ocean

Precise route unknown!

About 68 days after leaving Nova Albion the *Golden Hinde* finds land again. The ship's company is down to 62 men and boys. After a fight with the Palau Islanders, they sail on. Local fishermen guide Drake to the Moluccas, known as the Spice Islands. When Sultan Babú of Ternate is told that Drake represents the Queen of England, he meets Drake's ship in a great royal canoe and his people tow it into harbor.

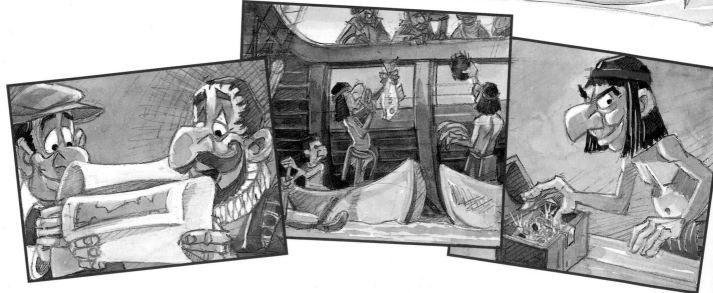

WITH THE AID OF SPANISH CHARTS from captured ships, the *Golden Hinde* sails away from America and heads west across the Pacific.

IN THE PALAU ISLANDS, about 100 canoes, full of native people come to trade coconuts, fish and fruit in return for beads. But the islanders then decide to

take what they want from the ship. Hundreds more return. Drake fires a cannon and about 20 natives are killed.

21

Sailing into Trouble

The next destination is the island of Java, 994 miles (1,600 km) further southwest, in the Indian Ocean. It is difficult to find a way through the many islands here and the *Golden Hinde* strikes a coral reef. She is stuck fast and the crew are worried. As darkness falls the ship could be smashed to pieces on the reef. In the hope that the tide will free the ship next day, Drake orders the crew to lighten the ship. Food, cannons and tons of cloves worth a fortune are thrown overboard! The next day, at four in the afternoon, the tide lifts the ship off the reef.

CRRunch!

DRAKE ORDERS YOU TO PRAY for them. Your sermon suggests that the disaster is God's punishment for the expedition's piracy and for the execution of Thomas Doughty. Drake is furious with you!

DRAKE ORDERS that you are to be tied up with a sign reading, 'Francis Fletcher, ye falseth knave that liveth'.

Homeward Bound

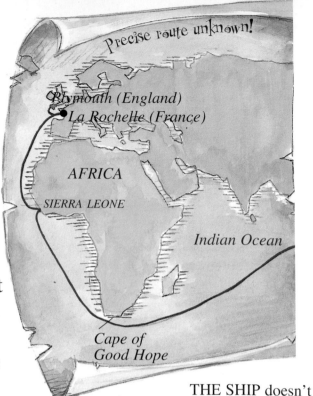

ou eventually reach Java, after strong winds blow the ship off course. You anchor on the south coast and send gifts to the local ruler, the raja. He gives you hens, coconuts and rice in return. Once again the ship is careened. You take on more supplies for the homeward journey — water, hens, goats, fruit and seven tons of rice! Portuguese spies find their way on board, taking notes on the state and contents of the *Golden Hinde*. Drake sets sail for the Cape of Good Hope.

Precise route unknown!

Plymouth (England)
La Rochelle (France)

AFRICA

SIERRA LEONE

Indian Ocean

Cape of Good Hope

THE SHIP doesn't touch land for over 80 days and only just makes it to Sierra Leone before you all die of thirst.

Home at Last!

DRAKE ANCHORS near La Rochelle, France. Some of the treasure is secretly unloaded — probably in case you get a hostile welcome in England for upsetting the Spanish so much!

THE *GOLDEN HINDE* finally sails back into Plymouth on September 26, 1580.

DRAKE'S WIFE, Mary, and the mayor of Plymouth come to see Drake on his ship. Messages are sent to the Queen in London, telling of his safe return.

25

Fame and Riches

Francis Drake's navigational skills are extraordinary. Only Magellan had ever circumnavigated the globe before — and he died on his homeward journey! However, despite his success, Queen Elizabeth keeps her distance from Drake. She knows that no sea captain has been more destructive to the Spanish empire. But she is curious to see Drake's treasure and spends hours with him hearing about the voyage. Eventually the treasure is taken to the Tower of London.

The Queen had invested £1,000 in the expedition and she receives £47,000 in return. Drake is allowed to keep £10,000. He buys a large estate, called Bucklands Abbey, north of Plymouth.

Hurrumph!

THE TREASURE brought home to England is vast: it includes more than ten tons of silver and about 110 pounds (50 kg) of gold. Drake took some treasure off his ships before landing in England, how much is unknown.

THE SPANISH are not happy about Drake's actions, especially as they seem to be approved by Queen Elizabeth. The King of Spain starts building an invincible fleet to fight the English. It will finally set sail in 1588.

Arise, *Sir Francis Drake.*

Handy Hint

As Queen, ask the French ambassador to knight Drake so the Spanish don't think you approve of his piracy!

27

Final Voyage

THE QUEEN GRANTS DRAKE his own coat of arms with the motto 'Sic parvis magna' — 'Greatness from small beginnings'.

What Happens Next...

Sir Francis Drake continues to fight the Spanish. In 1585 he holds the island of Sào Tiago to ransom and burns down its towns. His attacks on the ports of Cadiz and Corunna in Spain in 1587 become known as the 'singeing of the King of Spain's beard'. Over two days, Drake steals or sinks 38 ships at Cadiz. In 1588, Drake takes part in the attack on the Spanish Armada at Calais, led by Lord High Admiral Howard of Effingham. Bad weather forces the Armada back to Spain and many of their ships are wrecked in storms.

On Drake's final voyage in 1596, he is ill with dysentery for several days and dies at sea, off the coast of Panama. His body is placed in a lead coffin and buried at sea. He is about 54 years old.

QUEEN ELIZABETH officially recognizes Drake's feat of circumnavigation. In 1581 she orders that the *Golden Hinde* be put in dry dock for safe keeping (opposite).

THE QUEEN TAKES possession of all Drake's logbooks, maps and charts. They are never seen again. Due to the secrecy surrounding Drake's voyage, mapmakers aren't able to update existing maps.

It's the Spanish Armada, Sir Francis!

Handy Hint (for Drake)

Like Fletcher, produce a book based on your journal from the voyage. If it gives too much away it won't be published for years to come!*

*The World Encompassed by Sir Francis Drake is finally published in 1628.

Glossary

Brimstone The old word for sulfur.

Buccaneer A pirate who raided the Spanish-owned land and treasure fleets in South America and the Caribbean.

Careening To put a ship over on one side to clean or repair its hull.

Circumnavigate To sail completely around the world.

Colony A group of settlers in a new country.

Cooper A person who makes and repairs barrels.

Dysentery Disease causing severe diarrhea.

Gibbet A wooden frame where executed criminals were hung for public viewing.

Magellan, Ferdinand A Portuguese explorer who attempted to circumnavigate the globe in 1519.

Mariner A seaman; a person who earns his living by going to sea.

Mutiny A rebellion against those in authority, for example against the captain of a ship.

Navigator A person who can plot a route and direct a ship to follow that route.

New World The Americas.

Peso The currency of Spain.

Pilot A person who has the skill to guide a ship into and out of a port.

Pirate A person who robs from and steals ships.

Privateer A privately owned ship hired for war service by a government.

Sào Tiago One of the Cape Verde Islands off the west coast of Africa under Spanish control

Sermon A religious speech.

Spanish Main The southern part of the Caribbean Sea where Spanish treasure fleets sailed in the 16th and 17th centuries.`

Surgeon A person on board a ship who looks after the sick and wounded.

Ternate One of the islands making up the Moluccas, or Spice Islands, between Celebes and New Guinea.

Index

A
Alexandria, Egypt 5, 8
de Anton, Juan 14-15
Arica, Peru 14

B
Bacallaos, Strait of 14
Benedict, the 8
Bucklands Abbey 26

C
Cacafuego, the 14-15, 16
Cadiz, Spain 28
Cano 16
Cape of Good Hope 24
Capitiana, the 16
careening 10, 16, 18, 24, 30
circumnavigation 26, 28, 30
cloves 21, 22
cooper 10, 30
Corunna, Spain 28

D
death, of Francis Drake 28
Doughty, Thomas 8, 10-11, 13, 22
dysentery 28

E
Elizabeth, Queen of England 1, 6, 8, 12, 17, 18, 20, 24, 26, 28
Elizabeth, the 8, 10, 12

F
Fletcher, Francis 5, 6, 22, 29
food 11, 12, 16-17, 20, 24

G
gold 6, 15, 21, 26
Golden Hinde, the 10-11, 12, 14, 16, 17, 18, 20, 22, 24, 28

H
Hatton, Christopher 11

Hawkins, William 7
Henry VIII, King of England 1, 7
Howard of Effingham 28

J
Java 22, 24
journal, of Francis Fletcher 29

L
La Rochelle, France 24
Lima, Peru 14

M
Magellan, Ferdinand 10, 26, 30
Magellan, Strait of 8, 10, 12
Manila, the Philippines 16
maps 9, 12, 28
Marigold, the 8, 10, 13
Mary, the 10
Mary Tudor 1
Mocha 14
Mogador, Morocco 8
Moluccas 8, 20
mutiny 10, 30

N
Northwest Passage 8, 14
Nova Albion 18

P
Palau Islands 20
Pelican, the 8, 10-11
penguins 12
Peru 12, 14
Philip II, King of Spain 1, 6, 15, 26
piracy (pirates) 6, 30
Plymouth, England 5, 8, 24, 26
Port St. Julian 10
privateers 6, 30

R
raids 6, 8, 10, 14

S
São Tiago, Cape Verde Islands 9, 28, 30
scurvy 9
Sierra Leone 24
de Silva, Nuño 9
silver 6, 14-15, 17, 26
slaves 6
South America 6, 10, 12
Spain 1, 6, 8
Spanish Armada 28
Spanish Main 5, 30
Spice Islands (*see* Moluccas)
storms 10, 12-13
Sultan Babu of Ternate 20
Swan, the 8

T
treasure 24, 26
treasure fleets (ships) 1, 6, 8, 16

V
Valpariso, Peru 14

W
water (drinking) 24-25

Z
de Zárate, Don Francisco 16-17

32